12/2015

BOY SCOUT
MERIT BADGE SERIES

ENTREPRENEURSHIP

This pamphlet is based on a pamphlet
created by the Center for Entrepreneurial
Leadership Inc. at the Ewing Marion
Kauffman Foundation and is distributed
with the permission of the center.

"Enhancing our youths' competitive edge through merit badges"

BOY SCOUTS OF AMERICA®

Requirements

1. In your own words, define *entrepreneurship*. Explain to your merit badge counselor how entrepreneurs impact the U.S. economy.

2. Explain to your counselor why having good skills in the following areas is important for an entrepreneur: communication, planning, organization, problem solving, decision making, basic math, adaptability, technical and social skills, teamwork, and leadership.

3. Identify and interview an individual who has started a business. Learn about this person's educational background, early work experiences, where the idea for the business came from, and what was involved in starting the business. Find out how the entrepreneur raised the capital (money) to start the business, examples of successes and challenges faced, and how the business is currently doing (if applicable). Discuss with your counselor what you have learned.

4. Think of as many ideas for a business as you can, and write them down. From your list, select three ideas you believe represent the best opportunities. Choose one of these and explain to your counselor why you selected it and why you feel it can be successful.

5. Create a written business plan for your idea that includes all of the following:

   a. Product or Service

      (1) Describe the product or service to be offered.

      (2) Identify goals for your business.

35891
ISBN 978-0-8395-5008-2
©2013 Boy Scouts of America
2013 Second Printing

(3) Explain how you can make enough of the product or perform the service to meet your goals.

(4) Identify and describe the potential liability risks for your product or service.

(5) Determine what type of license, if any, you might need in order to sell or make your product or service.

b. Market Analysis

(1) Identify the types of people who would buy your product or service.

(2) Identify your business's competitors, and describe their strengths and weaknesses.

(3) Describe what makes your product or service unique.

c. Financial

(1) Determine how much money you will need to start your business, and identify how you will obtain the money.

(2) Determine the cost of offering your product or service and the price you will charge in order to make a profit.

(3) Describe what will happen with the money you make from the sales of your product or service.

    d. Personnel

        (1) Determine what parts of the business you will handle yourself, and describe your qualifications.

        (2) Determine whether you will need additional help to operate your business. If you will need help, describe the responsibilities and qualifications needed for the personnel who will fill each role.

    e. Promotion and Marketing

        (1) Describe the methods you will use to promote your business to potential customers.

        (2) Explain how you will utilize the Internet and social media to increase awareness of your product or service.

        (3) Design a promotional flier or poster for your product or service.

6. When you believe your business idea is feasible, imagine your business idea is now up and running. What successes and problems might you experience? How would you overcome any failures? Discuss with your counselor any ethical questions you might face and how you would deal with them.

Contents

Be Your Own Boss

If you have dreamed of going into business for yourself, you are not alone. Surveys show that more than half of American teenagers and college students are interested in starting their own businesses. Many new ventures are launched every day.

Starting a business is hard work. It also can be great fun. People launch businesses for many reasons: to work at something they love, to have the freedom to chart their own course, to be self-sufficient, and to have a chance for financial independence.

Making money, however, should never be a person's *only* reason for starting a business. People who go into business to "get rich quick" are seldom as successful as those who pursue their dreams with passion, commitment, and the necessary skills.

Build a business on something you love—an idea, a talent, an interest that captures your imagination and fires your enthusiasm—and you may feel you are not working at all. While you may actually work harder than you have ever worked at anything, you will be having too much fun to notice. Successful entrepreneurs do what they do because they love it. They are following a dream and having an adventure.

An entrepreneur is many things. Most are adventurous, self-reliant, and energetic, and they have other qualities you will learn about as you work on the Entrepreneurship merit badge. The common definition of an entrepreneur is "someone who operates a business." Thinking of an entrepreneur as a problem solver, however, may help you better understand what makes an entrepreneur tick.

Entrepreneurs are always looking for problems they can solve, gaps they can fill, or unmet needs they can answer with the right product or service. To sell their products or services, entrepreneurs often start businesses.

As you earn this merit badge you will look at what entrepreneurs do, their characteristics and skills, and how they bring new ideas, products, and services to people and society. You will learn about identifying opportunities, creating and evaluating business ideas, and exploring the feasibility (how doable it is) of an idea as you develop a basic business plan. You will also have the chance to fit everything together as you consider running your own business venture.

With a little imagination and the skills you learn as you earn the Entrepreneurship merit badge, you could start your own business, like the makers of the Willis Water Bomb, *above*.

Many Scouts who start a business to earn the Entrepreneurship merit badge will probably operate that business for only one to three months. Some of the areas covered in this pamphlet—especially the financial areas—may seem complicated when you first read about them. However, you will find that these are really not difficult to handle (and, in fact, can be fun) when starting up and running a small business for a short time.

As you work to complete the requirements for this merit badge, you will have done much of the hard work necessary to start a business. As you take each step, you may learn the joys of being your own boss and earning money by pursuing an interest or a passion. Working toward this merit badge might just help you create your own path to small-business success—and change your future!

Entrepreneurs can make a profitable business from just about any hobby. Timothy Johnson of Littleton, Colorado, owns Busy Bee Enterprises, which sells products made from honey. He continues to operate that business today.

What Do Entrepreneurs Do?

To understand what an entrepreneur is and does, start with the word "problem." Most people face problems every day. Problems frustrate, confuse, and annoy most people, unless those people happen to be entrepreneurs.

Every Problem Is an Opportunity

Entrepreneurs see problems as *opportunities.* When they come up against problems, they start looking for solutions. Entrepreneurs are problem solvers.

Think of some things people might want that are not readily available, such as:

- A toothbrush that brushes both sides of your teeth at the same time

- An umbrella that does not bend or break in a strong wind

- A way to eat chocolate on a hot day without its melting and making a mess

Because people's wants and needs are endless and always changing, resourceful entrepreneurs will always seek ways to meet those wants and needs. Entrepreneurs recognize opportunities and take action. They get excited by the challenge of finding solutions to problems.

The Entrepreneur's *NEWS*— Read All About It

The *NEWS* motivates entrepreneurs—the *N* stands for **needs.** **Events**—the *E*—motivate entrepreneurs, too. Entrepreneurs sometimes find opportunities when special events happen. If aliens were to land on Earth, you can be sure some enterprising entrepreneurs would see opportunities to create business ventures. Just think of the possibilities, from TV appearances and parades to creating and marketing space-alien action figures. The *W* stands for **wants.** Entrepreneurs are also motivated by the element of **surprise**—the *S*. Entrepreneurs love to surprise people with new ideas.

The Business of Doing Good

Many successful entrepreneurs are motivated by doing something they enjoy. Socially responsible entrepreneurs take that enjoyment one step further by making money while also feeling good about benefiting society. Succeeding as a social entrepreneur can depend on three factors:

- Linking the business and the issue it addresses. As an example, one company donates a pair of shoes to someone in need for each pair sold.

- Recognizing that a socially responsible business may not provide a quick return on investment. Because the emphasis of this kind of business is not just on making money, turning a profit may take longer.

- Believing in your goals will encourage others—employees, investors—to help you achieve them.

Many companies today place great value on social responsibility. One company, started in 1982 by a famous actor, has donated more than $370 million to charity. Another company, which produces sportswear and sports gear, is committed to environmentally responsible manufacturing processes and has given more than $55 million to environmental organizations.

As you explore ideas for your own business, consider whether social responsibility is a natural fit. When you discover what you love to do, you may be able to link your business to a cause you feel passionate about and do well while doing good.

What Is the Marketplace?

The *marketplace* is the entire "arena" of places where people can buy all sorts of goods and services. Identify a group of people who would want to buy a particular product or service, and you have identified a potential *market*. Whenever there is a potential market, there is an opportunity to start a business.

Products are something physical that you can touch. Products may go by other names such as "goods," "merchandise," or "items." Some examples of products include cars, clocks, clothes, food, jewelry, and baseball cards.

A *service* is useful work that does not produce a tangible (touchable) product. A haircut is an example of a service. Yes, you can touch hair, but you are paying for the service of having your hair cut. Other examples of services include tutoring, lawn mowing, dog walking, Web page design, and pool cleaning.

Edsel

Failure—It's Part of the Game

Failure is a fact of the entrepreneurial life. Some of the most famously successful entrepreneurs have had equally famous failures. The Edsel of the Ford Motor Company was a legendary flop. In the mid-80s, Coca-Cola introduced a beverage called "new Coke" to replace the original soft drink formula. New Coke was a disaster, and Coca-Cola eventually reintroduced the original soft drink as "Coca-Cola Classic." Don't let the possibility of failure stop you from pursuing your entrepreneurial dream. Entrepreneurs learn from their failures and use what they learn to excel at their next ventures.

The Power of Entrepreneurial Thinking

When entrepreneurs turn their ideas into businesses, they help the national economy grow. Through entrepreneurship, many Scouts may be able to improve the quality of their own lives as well as the quality of other people's lives. The United States has a history of encouraging individuals to realize their dreams through entrepreneurship.

Entrepreneurial talents also can be useful in many areas besides starting new business ventures. For example, some entrepreneurial thinkers start community programs, revitalize neighborhoods, or advise government agencies on how to solve specific problems. Entrepreneurs contribute to every aspect of society.

Identity five people you think are entrepreneurs. Why do you think they are entrepreneurs? How do they affect the lives of other people? What would not exist if it were not for their efforts?

Activity: What Is an Entrepreneur?

It is not easy to state exactly what an entrepreneur is, but give it a try. Entrepreneurs are creative and try to solve problems, so use this activity as an opportunity to be entrepreneurial; create a definition that works for you. Write your response.

A major motivator for successful entrepreneurs is the great feeling that comes from doing something they enjoy. Think about your own hobbies, favorite activities, and skills or talents. Perhaps you know more than the average person about some subject of interest. Your best business opportunities will come from the things you love to do and that interest you. Consider your own wants and needs, not just those of the marketplace.

Famous Names

Some of this country's best-known business operators are entrepreneurs. Some started small businesses to produce a product or service, and their businesses then grew into major corporations. Here is a handful of well-known ones.

Entrepreneur	Entrepreneurial Venture
Wally Amos	Famous Amos Chocolate Chip Cookie Company
Jeff Bezos	Amazon.com
Michael Dell	Dell Inc.
Emilio Estefan	Crescent Moon Recordings
Debra Fields	Mrs. Fields Inc.
David Filo, Jerry Yang	Yahoo! Inc.
Berry Gordy	Motown Record Corporation
David Karp	Tumblr
Tim Leatherman	Leatherman multi-tool
J. Willard Marriott	Marriott Corporation
Pierre Omidyar	eBay
Larry Page, Sergey Brin	Google
Mark Zuckerberg	Facebook

Wally Amos   **Larry Page, Sergey Brin**   **Michael Dell**

If you are willing to take well-considered risks to achieve a personal goal in starting a business, you may be a risk manager. Think about what might lead you to accept such risks.

Entrepreneurs: Their Roles and Contributions

When entrepreneurs begin a new venture, they risk losing their own money or money from investors. They risk losing the time and effort they have invested. They risk a loss of pride if their idea does not work. They risk losing their livelihood—their means of supporting themselves. If they have employees, their employees' jobs also are at risk.

It may seem that entrepreneurs are risk takers who enjoy danger. In fact, most entrepreneurs are risk *managers,* not risk seekers. A wise entrepreneur does not take foolish or reckless risks. Rather, entrepreneurs carefully consider potential risks, then weigh them against potential benefits and determine if a risk is worth taking.

Entrepreneurs who decide to pursue a venture enjoy the challenge of seeing if they can make it succeed. They thrive on challenge. The willingness to make decisions and take actions that involve risk is a key factor that distinguishes entrepreneurs from nonentrepreneurs.

Crazy — or Visionary?

Entrepreneurs sometimes pursue ideas that others think are crazy. Some entrepreneurs may try business ideas so strange, they cannot succeed. However, they may become highly successful by pursuing unusual opportunities that others have dismissed, overlooked, or found too challenging. If and when these entrepreneurs succeed, the same people who predicted failure will view them as visionaries—pioneers who had great insight about the future.

Job Generators

People also respect entrepreneurs because they create opportunities for others. Entrepreneurs typically gather teams of people who help make their visions reality. In doing so, a successful entrepreneur serves as an important "growth engine" for our economy. Many operate small businesses, employing one to 20 people. Some have grown into huge corporations employing thousands of workers. Thus, entrepreneurs are responsible for creating large numbers of jobs as well as providing goods and services that people want.

Entrepreneurs deserve the respect they get. They see opportunities rather than problems. They seek solutions. They accept risks, investing their time, talent, energy, and money to produce goods and services that improve people's lives. In the process, they create opportunities for others. For all of these reasons, entrepreneurs are important contributors to society.

People respect entrepreneurs for accepting risks and producing goods and services others want and will buy. They respect entrepreneurs for always thinking about how things *could* be instead of being satisfied with the way things *are*.

Entrepreneurs: Key Characteristics and Skills

While entrepreneurs have in common certain characteristics and skills, great individuality exists among them. In sports, some athletes do well because they love their sport, have developed their skills, and are trained. Others show natural talent and require less training.

In much the same way, some entrepreneurs get formal training. Others have a natural flair for entrepreneurship. Still others succeed despite taking highly unusual approaches.

The Successful Entrepreneur

Here are several important personal characteristics and attitudes many effective entrepreneurs seem to share.

Do What You Love. The successful entrepreneur has **passion.** People who feel committed to and care deeply about what they do stand the best chance of being successful at it. The heart and mind must be allies. Entrepreneurs typically care more about what they do than how much money they might make. The amount they earn is often secondary to achieving their goals.

Believe in Yourself. Another key quality of the successful entrepreneur is **self-confidence.** Do you have confidence in your ability to succeed? Every entrepreneur faces problems, and you must believe you can overcome them.

Look to the Future. Entrepreneurs create a **vision** of their future, and then they work to achieve it. To accomplish their goals and make their vision a reality, successful entrepreneurs must have **drive** and a willingness to work hard. They must have persistence and the ability to complete tasks. They must keep trying.

Additionally, entrepreneurs are **opportunity-focused** and **forward-looking.** They are able to set both short- and long-term goals. These are some of the qualities that help entrepreneurs see problems as opportunities.

Accept the Challenges. Entrepreneurs have a high **tolerance for risk.** Their self-confidence helps them accept the challenges of the path they take.

If you feel you lack self-confidence, you might not fully appreciate your past accomplishments. Think about all the things you have done—took part in music, art, or sports; advanced in rank and earned merit badges in Scouting; and held positions of responsibility in your troop or at school. Have you held a part-time job? Do you regularly help out at home? You will find you have every right to be self-confident. Successful entrepreneurs believe they are capable of success and that they are *worthy* of success.

> Believe in your ability to be creative. Experts say the biggest block to creativity is thinking that you are not creative.

Entrepreneurs tend to **thrive on competition.** While they may actively compete with others, they are more likely to compete against themselves. They are constantly trying to improve their own performance.

Be Innovative. Although they might not realize it, most entrepreneurs are **creative.** They find innovative ways to solve problems. They always look for new and better ways to do things—ways that have not occurred to others.

Keep Learning. Entrepreneurs are **willing to learn.** They might already know a great deal, yet they recognize that no one knows everything and they can learn valuable information from others. Entrepreneurs who are open to listening and learning will enhance their ability to achieve success.

Is Entrepreneurship for Everybody?

Not everyone has the qualities to be an entrepreneur, or even wants to be an entrepreneur. Even a person who has the necessary qualities is not automatically made happy by being an entrepreneur. Some people who have entrepreneurial characteristics are often happier working for someone else.

If you have some of the characteristics discussed here but you do not feel drawn to becoming an entrepreneur, you can find ways to further your goals or your chosen career by putting your entrepreneurial characteristics to work for you. It may surprise you how much recognition you will get for the good work you do.

Activity: Are You a Potential Entrepreneur?

Part 1: Entrepreneurial Characteristics—Personal Review and Assessment

On a scale of 1 to 10, rate yourself on the following characteristics, with a "1" meaning "strongly disagree" and a "10" meaning "strongly agree." Record your score on a separate sheet of paper.

I am a person who

1. Is passionate, with strong feelings about things personally important to me

2. Is self-confident

3. Has high self-esteem

4. Is capable of accomplishing whatever I set out to do

5. Is self-reliant

6. Is opportunity-oriented

7. Is forward-thinking

8. Has vision and goals

9. Has drive and ambition

10. Is willing to work hard

11. Is willing to take a risk

12. Is competitive, especially against myself

13. Is creative

14. Is willing to learn

Total your score. If you score more than 100, you are a good candidate for entrepreneurship. Then again: If you score less than 100, you may also be a good candidate for entrepreneurship. Remember, there is no set formula for who can or cannot be a successful entrepreneur. The purpose of this activity is to help you explore your interest in and abilities for entrepreneurship.

Everything Has an "Opportunity Cost"

Like most successful people, entrepreneurs carefully consider their *opportunity cost*. For example, when they commit time and money to a venture, they cannot commit that same time and money to another opportunity. They must determine where it is wisest to invest their time and money.

Opportunity cost is an important consideration for just about anyone. For example, while you have been reading this, you could have been hanging out with friends, fixing a snack, playing sports, or getting ready for a camping trip. By choosing to read this pamphlet, you decided this was the best use of your time. The next best thing you could have done with your time (that is, your next best alternative, which you gave up) is your opportunity cost of reading this pamphlet and thinking about your entrepreneurial potential.

Few entrepreneurs possess every skill needed to ensure business success. They often look to experts for help in areas such as strategic planning, accounting, contracts, legal issues, and specialized marketing.

Some Entrepreneurial Skills for Success

Having the right attitude and characteristics can carry you only so far. You also need the *skills* that will help you succeed. However, unlike personal characteristics and attitude—which often can be hard or impossible to change—skills can be acquired if entrepreneurs are willing to learn them. Also, entrepreneurs can hire people who have the needed skills. Either way, the following skills are important if the entrepreneur's business is going to succeed.

Ability to Plan. Planning is a key skill. Entrepreneurs must be able to develop plans to meet goals in various areas including finance, marketing, production, sales, and personnel (hiring and keeping productive and satisfied employees).

Communication Skills. Entrepreneurs should be able to explain, discuss, sell, and market their product or service. You must be able to work effectively with your business team. Entrepreneurs need to be able to express themselves clearly, both verbally and in writing. They also should have strong reading comprehension skills to understand contracts and other forms of written business communication.

Marketing Skills. The success of a business depends very much on whether the business reaches the market (its potential customers), interests the market, and convinces customers to buy. Many entrepreneurs who failed started with an innovative product or service that, with proper marketing, could have been highly successful.

Good marketing skills—including hands-on demonstrations of a product—are critical for success.

Interpersonal Skills. Entrepreneurs constantly interact with people, including customers and clients, employees, financial lenders, investors, lawyers, and accountants, to name a few. The entrepreneur's ability to form and keep positive relationships is crucial to the success of the entrepreneur's business venture.

Basic Management Skills. Many entrepreneurs manage every part of their business. But even when entrepreneurs hire managers to attend to daily details, they must understand if their business has the right resources and if those *resources* are being used effectively. They must ensure that all the positions in their company are held by effective people.

Resources are the different elements that must be combined to produce a business product or offer a service. Resources may include money; equipment, supplies, and ingredients; personnel (workers, managers); work space; support services; transportation; and technology, knowledge, and information.

Personal Effectiveness. To handle the pressures of their busy lifestyles, entrepreneurs must be able to manage time well and to take care of personal business efficiently. Because first impressions are so important, entrepreneurs must also pay attention to such things as personal grooming, telephone skills, and being on time.

Think of the difference in the impression made by someone who answers the phone with "Yeah?" versus someone who says, "Acme Company, this is Alex. How may I help you?"

Team-Building Skills. Because entrepreneurs usually assemble a team of skilled people who help them achieve business success, they must be able to effectively develop and manage the team.

Leadership Skills. A key leadership skill for all entrepreneurs is the ability to develop a vision for the company and inspire the company associates to pursue that vision as a team. The expression "People would rather be led than managed" applies especially well to an entrepreneurial venture.

Think about the skills necessary to be a successful entrepreneur. What are your strong areas? In what areas would you most likely need help from other experts? Entrepreneurs must be able to realistically evaluate their own skills, and to know when to draw on the skills of others.

Activity: Are You a Potential Entrepreneur?

Part 2: Entrepreneurial Skills—Personal Review and Assessment

On a scale of 1 to 10, rate your skill in each area, with a "1" meaning the least amount of skill and a "10" meaning highly skilled. Record your score on a separate sheet of paper.

1. Ability to plan effectively
2. Spoken communication skills
3. Written communication skills
4. Reading skills
5. Marketing ability
6. Interpersonal skills
7. Basic management ability
8. Personal effectiveness
9. Team-building skills
10. Leadership ability

A score of 70 or higher means you might already have many of the key skills you need to be a successful entrepreneur. If you gave yourself a score of 6 or below on any of these items, you might want to work to improve that skill. If you are determined, you can improve any skill you believe you will need to become a successful entrepreneur.

Entrepreneurial Opportunities

Finding just the right opportunity takes time and research.

Identifying Entrepreneurial Opportunities

Now that you understand the qualities and skills successful entrepreneurs must have, consider entrepreneurial possibilities that might be right for you.

Find the Right Starting Place. Sometimes a great idea for a business will pop into an entrepreneur's head and the entrepreneur will run with it. Entrepreneurs want ideas to carry forward their hopes, dreams, and aspirations. However, rather than simply trying to come up with a good idea, an entrepreneur might want to focus on an *opportunity.* Opportunities are all around, so don't wait for someone else to do something about them.

Cast a Wide Net. Not all opportunities are worth pursuing. Before you decide that a particular opportunity is right for you, compile a list of possible opportunities. Think of every problem, need, want, event, and new possibility that you can. Do not worry at this point about whether something seems too hard, too easy, too large, or too small.

Activity: Hunting for Opportunities

Identify at least five opportunities—problems, needs, wants, events, surprises, or "gaps." Briefly describe each one with a note about where you found each opportunity. Rate the potential for each opportunity by giving it a score of 1 to 10, with 10 for the strongest potential. Identify your three highest-rated opportunities—the three you believe are the best for you. Think carefully about the reasons you use to rank one above another.

Look for opportunities everywhere—at the mall, in your neighborhood, at home, on the Internet, at school, on TV, or in magazines and newspapers. Look for the gaps—the unmet needs, the persistent problems, and the desirable things that do not yet exist.

Let your creativity and energy flow freely, and you may be surprised by how many opportunities you find. Do not evaluate them yet. Just find them. To help you spot opportunities, complete the following statements:

> *I wish there was a . . .*
>
> *I've always been bothered by . . .*
>
> *This would be much better if . . .*
>
> *This would be more fun if . . .*
>
> *This would not hurt so much if . . .*
>
> *This would not be so hard if . . .*
>
> *What this place needs is . . .*

Think of other statements or questions that can help you find opportunities. Talk to people about their needs and wants. Find out what they need help with, what they are too busy to do, what they don't like to do, or what they need more—or less—of.

Evaluating Entrepreneurial Opportunities

Finding an opportunity does not mean you should automatically pursue it. *Evaluate* it to determine whether it is the right opportunity for you.

- Do you have a strong desire to pursue this opportunity? Does it grab you?

- Do you have the ability to pursue it?

- Is there a large enough market for this opportunity?

- Can you pursue it without traveling too far?

- Will it be an ongoing opportunity, or is it short-term?

- How much are the start-up costs, and how much risk is involved?

You evaluate opportunities to judge how good they are and to compare them so you can decide which opportunities are best for you. Here are some things to think about as you evaluate the opportunities you have identified.

Have the Interest. Are you enthusiastic about the opportunity? Entrepreneurs must have a strong interest in the business area they choose. If you are not interested in what you are doing, you may be limiting how well you can or how long you want to do it.

Get the Knowledge. Do you know enough about it to pursue this opportunity? Occasionally, entrepreneurs successfully develop an opportunity they know nothing about. However, the more they know, the greater their chance of success. So, learn all you can about your opportunity.

Question Yourself. Still other questions to ask yourself include:

1. Do I have a good chance of developing a potentially successful business idea (either a product or a service) for this opportunity?

2. Would enough people actually be willing to purchase a product or a service to satisfy the problem, event, surprise, or unmet need that I see as an opportunity?

3. What risk do I run that other entrepreneurs will also see the opportunity and will become my competitors?

4. How strong are the existing competitors (if any) who are already trying to meet the problem, event, surprise, or unmet need?

5. Can I effectively market a product or service for this opportunity?

6. How expensive will it be to pursue this opportunity? What are my chances of making enough sales to cover costs, and of the business succeeding?

7. If I start a business around this opportunity, what are the chances that there will be a market for my product for a long time? Or am I addressing a temporary problem, event, surprise, or need?

8. Do I have enough information to decide whether this is an opportunity worth pursuing? How accurate is my information?

Activity: Rethinking Your Choices

Now, using the ways of evaluating opportunities that have been discussed, decide again what you think are the three best opportunities from your list of five or more. On a sheet of paper, make two columns. Title one column **Previous Top Three Opportunities** and title the other column **Current Top Three Opportunities**. In the first column, list the top three opportunities you chose at the end of the last section. In the second column, list the three you selected in this section.

Compare the two lists. If the top three opportunities you selected in this section are different from the top three you chose previously, what made you change your mind?

INTERVIEW AN ENTREPRENEUR

By now you have realized that entrepreneurs are all around you in your community. Find one who is willing to be interviewed. Typically, entrepreneurs are generous about sharing what they know with interested young people. By finding out how the entrepreneur selected an opportunity, identified the best idea to meet the opportunity, and made the idea into a business, you will develop insights into how to choose your own best opportunity.

The following are some sample questions you may want to ask the entrepreneur you interview. You may also ask the entrepreneur general questions about anything covered so far. Developing some of your own questions would be the entrepreneurial thing to do.

Sample Questions for the Entrepreneur You Interview

1. When did you start thinking about becoming an entrepreneur, and why did you want to be an entrepreneur?

2. What factors or who influenced you to want to become an entrepreneur?

3. What are the most important entrepreneurial characteristics and skills you think you possess?

4. What were your biggest obstacles in becoming an entrepreneur?

5. What problem, event, surprise, or unmet need did you identify as an opportunity?

6. What made you believe it was a good opportunity, and what business idea (product or service) did you come up with to address this opportunity?

7. How did you come up with your idea and know it was a good idea?

8. How did you identify and research your target market and your competition?

9. What problems did you have getting started, and how did you overcome them?

10. What kinds of expenses did you have when you started your business? What, if any, problems did you have raising enough capital (money) for your business?

11. Where did you get the money to start your business?

12. What surprises did you encounter in starting your business?

13. How did you find the best people to be part of your business team?

14. What ideas and approaches did you use to market your product or service? What approaches worked best and why?

15. Did you try any marketing approaches that did not work well? Why did they not work?

16. How well has your business performed in the past, and how well is it doing now?

17. Why do you think enough people will want to buy your product or service?

18. What advice would you offer to a young, potential entrepreneur like me?

19. What is your opinion of the three entrepreneurial opportunities I have identified, and which opportunity do you think is the best and why?

20. What advice can you offer me if I decide to pursue this opportunity?

Activity: The Interview

Using the suggested questions as a guide, develop your own questionnaire on a separate sheet of paper. Have at least 12 questions to ask a local entrepreneur. Be sure to include questions that will help you evaluate your three best opportunities. You may use any of the sample questions you think will be helpful. You may also create your own questions. When you have finished inter- viewing your selected entrepreneur, write a short report (or report in person to your counselor) on what you learned about the entrepreneur and about your three best opportunities.

Interview with an Entrepreneur

Name :
Business :

Questions

1. When did you start thinking about becoming an entrepreneur?

2. What problem or unmet need did you identify as an opportunity?

3. What business idea (good or service) did you come up with to address this opportunity?

4. How did you come up with your idea?

5. Where did you get the money to start your business?

6. What ideas did you use to market your good or service?

Generating and Evaluating Ideas

The best opportunity in the world will pass you by if you can't come up with a realistic idea for a product or service to take advantage of the opportunity. Your challenge now is to hatch specific and *marketable* product ideas to meet the opportunities you have selected.

Opportunities and Ideas Go Together

Assume for the moment that your grandparents, who live nearby, love to garden and have many flowers, shrubs, fruits, and vegetables in their yard. They tell you they would like to take a long summer vacation—three weeks or more. However, they are not comfortable asking their neighbors to water and weed for them, nor do they want to lose all the hard work they have put into their yard. You are glad to care for their shrubs and plants. You also realize that other people in their neighborhood and nearby have the same problem and do not have anyone to help them.

Voilà! You see a problem—an opportunity. You can probably come up with a business idea that will turn this problem into a profitable entrepreneurial venture.

Always think carefully about any opportunity you are considering and what is *really* needed to satisfy it. People sometimes generate ideas that miss important parts of the opportunities they have identified.

For example, if you decide to specialize in the plant-watering business but do not include weeding as part of your service, your business idea will not solve your grandparents' problem or the potentially similar problems of other people nearby. Your business idea would probably not be able to take good advantage of the opportunity you identified because it missed an important part of the opportunity—the need for weeding.

Generating Ideas: How to Turn On the Tap

Here are some suggestions that may spark your creativity in developing good business ideas.

1. Seek out creative people and ask them about your business ideas. Their different points of view may help you explore new possibilities.

2. Try to view your opportunity in out-of-the-ordinary ways. Good business ideas often come from finding new solutions to old problems.

3. Spend time daydreaming. Letting your mind wander can produce interesting results. Research has shown that people are more creative when they are having fun. An afternoon of recreational sports or a trip down a waterslide might free your creative side.

4. Link one opportunity to others. If you are going to take care of gardens, what other services might you offer homeowners who will be away? Picking up the newspaper and mail, caring for pets, watering and/or mowing the lawn, watering indoor plants, and checking house security daily are other services for which homeowners might be willing to pay.

Try this creative-thinking exercise: Consider two seemingly unrelated things (a military tank and a swimming pool, for example), and think of a way they could be brought together and linked.

Hot Opportunities for Teen Entrepreneurs

Here are a few examples of businesses that have been started and operated successfully by young entrepreneurs. As you can see, the possibilities are many. This list may help *you* find the right business idea.

Advertising flier delivery service

Auto detailing

Bike repair

Boat and RV cleaning

Computer servicing/repair/upgrading/software installation

Desktop publishing

Errand-running service

Foreign-language translation or tutoring

Handcrafts (artworks, fishing lures, greeting cards, jewelry, metalwork, pottery, sculptures, shell crafts, T-shirts, wood carvings, etc.)

House-sitting

Lawn and plant care/gardening

Pet care/pet grooming/pet-sitting/dog walking/aquarium cleaning/cage and stall cleaning

Photography

Pool cleaning

Snow removal

Sports coaching

Tutoring

Web page design

Window cleaning

Go to the Source

Now that you have some techniques for generating ideas, select the three best potential business ideas (goods or services) for your three best opportunities. Then evaluate your potential ideas. Find the best "partnership" you can between opportunity and business idea. A key step is finding your *target markets*— that is, the potential customers who are most likely to buy or use the products or services that come from your ideas.

The starter list of questions will help you evaluate your different ideas for products and services. Some are questions to ask yourself; others are questions you may want to ask potential customers (or other entrepreneurs). You will think of many more questions to help you pinpoint your best idea.

Questions to ask yourself:

1. Has this idea been tried before? If not, why not? If this idea has been tried, was it successful? Can I improve upon it?

2. Will my idea let me compete successfully? Why would people buy my product instead of my competitor's product?

3. What information helped me come up with this idea? How confident am I of the accuracy and reliability of that information?

4. Do I have a good chance of finding enough money to start a business based on this idea?

5. Do I have enough personal time to create and run a business based on this idea? If not, can I find enough help?

Activity: Customer Interview and Business Idea Evaluation

Interview potential customers about your three best ideas. Report what you learn. Based on all of your information so far, identify the *best idea* you have found.

A unit is one item for sale, such as a T-shirt or a wood carving, or in the case of a service business that charges by the hour, one hour of the service provided. You will learn more about units and how to set a price per unit later in this pamphlet.

Questions to ask potential customers or other entrepreneurs:

1. Do you like my business idea? Why or why not? (If you have a prototype, show it to your potential customer or to the entrepreneur.)

2. Would you be willing to buy my business product? Why or why not?

3. At what price would you be willing to buy one unit of my business product?

4. How many units would you be willing to buy at alternative (different) prices? (List the possible prices you might charge, from high to low.)

5. Do you think my business product is better than that of my competitors? Why or why not?

6. Do you think this product (or service) will be too expensive to produce (or provide)? Do you think I will be able to make enough sales of this product to keep a business running successfully?

7. What could I do to improve my business product that would encourage you to buy more or pay a higher price for the same product or service?

8. Do you think the market for my business product will last long enough for it to be worth my starting a business?

Getting Down to Business: The Plan

Having an idea for a business and starting a business are two different things. Once you have what you believe is a good idea, the next step is to explore its *feasibility* as an actual business venture—not only to convince yourself that your idea will work, but also to convince others. If you will need money from other people to start your business, they will want to see evidence that the business has a good likelihood of succeeding. In most cases, they will want to see a *business plan.*

The Business Plan

A business plan organizes your business idea on paper. It helps other people *and you* understand the resources and steps needed to create your business, and its chances for success once it is started. A business plan is useful because it will:

- Be helpful in securing funding from most financial sources, including family and friends

- Help you think through all of the various aspects of the business and develop confidence that your idea is a good one

- Serve as a guide once the business is up and operating

Developing a business plan should be fun and enjoyable. It is, after all, the plan for how you will accomplish something you think is important and beneficial to others as well as to yourself. Developing a plan usually takes a great deal of research, thinking, and writing. You probably will end up talking with many people and going to many places, such as libraries, government sources, and professional associations.

The following outlines some key points to cover in your basic business plan. If you work your way through this outline as a general guide, you will find out most of what you need to know to determine whether your idea is likely to become a successful business.

Use this outline if you find it helpful, but do not think that you *must* follow it. Change it. Improve on it. Make your plan work for your business idea.

There is no magic formula for a business plan. Businesses are very different from one another, as are entrepreneurs. As a result, plans will vary.

Business Plan

Section 1: Describe the Business

- What is the name of your business?

- What are your business goals?

- What product or service do you plan to sell?

- Where will the business be located? What are its hours of operation? (Give the company address and phone, fax, website, and email address, as applicable.)

Section 2: Describe the Personnel

- What skills and experiences will help make your business idea work?

- What skills and experiences do you bring to the business?

- In what areas will you need help?

- Who will help you? (Describe positions for the different tasks that will need to be done to run the business, and describe the experiences and skills required of the people who will fill those positions. If you already have people in mind, name them.)

Section 3: Describe the Market and Your Competition

- Who are your main customers (your target market)?

- Why do customers need your product? (Name the chief benefits of the product or service your company will produce.)

- How will you set a price for your product?

- Who are your competitors?

- What are your company's competitive advantages? (How does your product or service differ from that of your competitors? How is it better or unique?)

- What sales tools will you use? (How will you convince customers to buy your product or service?)

- What are your sales goals?

Section 4: Describe Your Finances

- What items do you need to start your business?

- How much will each item cost?

- Where do you plan to get the money to cover your start-up costs?

- What is your estimated income (revenue) for four or six weeks?

- What are your estimated expenses (cash paid out) for those same weeks?

- How will you keep records of income, expenses, and profits?

Section 5: Provide Supporting Information

- Customer surveys

- Market research

- Promotional tools—sample advertising fliers, business cards, etc.

Marketing for Success

Once your business plan is complete, design a marketing plan that informs potential customers about your product or service. Get started by defining the following.

1. My target market is _____ .
   Consider the type of people who will be your customers, including their needs and ways you can help fill those needs.

2. My primary sales message is _____ .
   Simply state the main reason a customer would want your product or service. This message may incorporate your advantages over any competitors.

3. My secondary sales message is _____ .
   This statement conveys an additional benefit. Keep your primary and secondary sales messages brief and to the point.

4. My best sales tools and promotions will be _____ .
   Consider fliers, brochures, posters, websites, advertising, publicity, and one-on-one sales calls for disseminating your sales message. Promotions might include coupons, special events, free samples, and more.

5. Social media I can use include _____ .
   Think about ways to put social media tools (with your parent's permission) such as Facebook, Twitter, or Instagram to work to promote your business. For example, if you have a landscape company, you might post on Facebook before-and-after photos of lawns you service. Or you might share positive customer comments about your product or service on Twitter.

Keep these recommendations in mind:

- If you use photos of customers or their property in your social media marketing, make sure to first obtain their permission in writing.

- Limit your social media marketing to a few outlets so you will have time to adequately manage the ones you do use.

- Use social media to build your sales. For example, you might want to reward a customer "like" on Facebook with a free added-value item with their next purchase. Or you could begin a "yard of the month" contest among your lawn care clients: Offer a free week of service for the yard that receives the most votes on Twitter, and a free estimate for each potential customer who votes.

- Tailor your medium to your audience. For example, women are more active than men are on Pinterest, and many business people are adept at utilizing LinkedIn.

Be Prepared!

The Scout motto, *Be Prepared,* applies particularly well to the entrepreneur. Even if you discover later that you must change direction, you will adjust more effectively to the change if you have a plan that is guiding you. Having a plan will give you a greater sense of control and direction over your future and the future of your business.

Many business plans are short and have fewer than 25 pages, although the length will vary with the type of business. You might decide to start with a very simple business idea with a plan only five to 10 pages long. That is fine.

Love It? You Might Have to Leave It

Be prepared to be completely honest with yourself. Perhaps you have come up with a great idea. Maybe you love the prospect of running the business you are trying to create. However, if your research and plan indicate that the business will not work, you must recognize the need to change course.

Changing course does not necessarily mean abandoning your idea. It might mean only that you must modify the idea or approach it differently. However, if your research shows that your idea simply will not work, do not proceed with "launch." Many entrepreneurs fail because they refuse to accept that an interesting idea might not work as a profitable business.

If your review of the plan leads you to believe your idea *will* work, test it with people whom you respect or who have experience in similar business areas. Their views will be particularly valuable if you will be seeking resources from others to help start and initially operate your business.

These friendly reviewers can give you an idea of how others will likely react to your plan. Ask them to be brutally honest, not just polite. Tell them that if they foresee a problem, you want to know about it, without sugarcoating, so you can address it.

Make sure your business plan contains all of the information needed to convince you that the business will succeed, and to convince others of the same.

Jon Walker of Golden, Colorado, works on the business end of his sales venture. His product, Ding Dog™, is marketed as a way to let dog owners "know when their dog has to go."

Business Basics

Now consider a few more basics of business and entrepreneurship as you establish your business plan.

Setting Goals: Be SMART!

Having goals is important for you personally, and important for a business. There is an old saying: "If you don't know where you are going, you are sure to get there." In other words, you might end up nowhere if you do not decide where you want to go and focus on trying to reach that specific goal.

In setting goals, consider the following things:

Specific. Be as specific as you can. If you plan to take a trip, for example, and someone asks you "Where to?" and you reply, "Out West," you have named a general goal but not a specific destination. "Out West" could mean Seattle, Los Angeles, the Grand Canyon, or many other places. Your experience at one place would be quite different from your experience at another.

The same is true of a business. If you have only a general goal, you could end up at any one of several different "places" or business situations. It is hard to make decisions about how to reach your goal when you don't have a clear goal.

Entrepreneurs often must make quick decisions, in the middle of confusion, and based on vague or even contradictory information. Understanding your goals clearly and precisely can help guide your actions and decisions.

Measurable. As much as you can, make your goals something you can measure. That will help you know how far along you are and when you have achieved your goals.

On a trip, it helps you to know, for example, that your destination is 1,400 miles away and there are certain cities and landmarks through which you should expect to pass in a particular order. Similarly, for your business goals, it helps to know how far you have to go, what to look for on your way there, and how to tell when you have arrived.

You do not have to attach numbers to all of your goals. If one of your goals is to have fun, that would be hard to measure. If one of your goals is to enjoy working with the people on your team and helping them feel a sense of accomplishment, that also would be hard to measure.

Attainable. A goal can be challenging, but you should be able to envision how you can reach it. To be attainable, a goal should fit your personality, your values, your priorities, and your dreams and aspirations. Under-stand what can be achieved in the business you plan to start and run. If the steps to reaching that goal fit with the expectations you set for yourself, then your goal   is attainable.

Relevant. All your goals need to relate to achieving your vision of starting and running your own business, no matter how large or small they are. If the goal is not connected to reaching the vision, it probably isn't necessary.

Timely. Set goals for various "time horizons"—short-term, medium-term, and long-term. Make them interesting enough to motivate and inspire you, and space them so you can feel ongoing satisfaction as you achieve them. Set realistic timelines for your goals. These do not have to be precise, but you should identify what goals you hope to achieve in (for example) three weeks, six weeks, six months, one year, or five years from when you start. Timelines will help you chart your course, check your progress, and make decisions.

As you can see, the letters SMART make a handy way to remember the main points just discussed.

Aim for goals that have reasonable targets—not too easy, not too hard, but difficult enough to motivate you, inspire you, and provide a real sense of satisfaction once you have achieved them.

To Market, to Market

When you discover an idea for a product or service, based on an opportunity you have identified, you must consider the nature of the market to which your business will be targeted. In some cases, an entrepreneur might try to develop a new market for a brand-new product or service. In many cases, existing markets have opportunities for entrepreneurs because there is not enough of a particular product or service available, or customers want an improved, less expensive, or more convenient or accessible version of an existing product or service.

The DeLorean

Consider the car market. Why do so few entrepreneurs enter the car market today? In the early 1980s, a carmaker named John DeLorean tried to produce a new line of cars. If you saw the movie *Back to the Future,* maybe you noticed that a souped-up DeLorean car was used as a special-effects automobile for "time travel." Despite that moment of fame in the movies, the DeLorean was not successful in the automobile market. Entering the car market today is extremely expensive. It requires a massive amount of financial investment in many areas including design, production facilities, and major advertising and promotion campaigns. A brand-new car manufacturer would also face stiff competition and have a big challenge convincing customers to purchase its product—as DeLorean discovered.

> Because business markets vary so much, a key challenge for new entrepreneurs is to choose the best market to enter, and to avoid markets with too many obstacles.

This example shows that some markets are hard to enter because of the high start-up costs required. It also illustrates how difficult it is to compete with the strength of existing producers. Markets may be difficult to enter because they are already crowded with strong sellers.

On the other hand, markets can be too small for entrepreneurs to enter successfully. For example, an entrepreneur might try to start a computer-cleaning service in a small town, only to discover that there are not enough people with computers, or who want their computers cleaned, to support the business.

The level and quality of competition, and start-up costs are just some of the ways in which markets can vary. Therefore, as you consider your business idea, scrutinize the nature of the market your business will enter. Some markets may be more suited to you than others or may offer a better chance of success than others. Try to identify a target market in which you believe you will have your best competitive opportunity for generating sales, based on your knowledge, observations, experiences, and market research.

Fun With Financials

Financial considerations are essential to a business. It takes money to start a business, and every business will face different kinds of costs. For starters, the business will always need enough cash available to pay its bills and meet its other financial obligations. Eventually, a company will earn profits (or so its owners hope).

You, the entrepreneur—as well as your partners, lenders, and investors—will want to have financial information about your company that will help you understand the costs of starting the business and its prospects for earning profits. The following describes some basic financial information that a new business typically provides in its business plan and (where appropriate) continues to track as the company moves into operation.

Start-Up Costs

To figure your start-up costs, you total the amount of money you will need to get your business up and running. These costs are for only the initial start-up period of your business. Costs might include starting expenses for items such as rent for office or shop space, telephone, equipment, advertising and marketing, supplies and labor for the first units you will produce, and insurance.

As an entrepreneur, you estimate your start-up costs to help determine whether it makes financial sense to start your business. Your estimate will also help you predict how much money, if any, you will need from others to start the business.

Costs of Getting Started

Copy the chart on the next page. Change it as required to include the items you will need for your business's first two weeks. Indicate how you will get each item—by purchasing, renting, borrowing, bartering, or through a donation. (*Bartering* is trading—you trade a product or service in exchange for a product or service you need. A donation is a gift—somebody gives you the needed item.) For those items that cost money, write in an estimated amount of cash.

Many entrepreneurs try to keep start-up costs as low as they can. This practice is sometimes referred to as "bootstrapping" a business. (Launching a full-fledged business with tiny start-up costs can be like pulling on heavy boots using small loops, or "bootstraps"—hence the idea of bootstrapping a business.)

Item	Cost	Purchase	Rent	Borrow	Barter	Donation
Telephone						
Transportation:						
Bike						
Bus fare						
Car (gas, oil, etc.)						
Equipment						
Bookkeeping supplies						
Advertising/ marketing						
Bank account (cost of service fees)						
Product cost; materials						
Labor						
Attorney/legal fees						
Filing costs (for registering company)						
Consumable supplies (used while providing service)						
Other:						

Figure the total cash you will need for the first two weeks of your business by adding the costs of all items you have listed to purchase or rent.

Total cash needed for start-up: $ _____

©1996 Marilyn Kourilsky. Adapted from M. Kourilsky, *Mini-Society: Entrepreneurship—Debriefing Teachable Moments* (Center for Entrepreneurial Leadership, 1996). Used by permission of Marilyn Kourilsky.

Your list tells you that, in addition to the items you will get by borrowing, by bartering, or through donations, you will need $ _____ IN CASH to start your business and operate it for at least two weeks. Indicate the sources you will rely on to get the cash.

Source	Amount
Personal savings	$ _____
Borrow from family	$ _____
Borrow from friends	$ _____
Borrow from bank	$ _____
Partner's savings (if applicable)	$ _____
Earnings from first two weeks of business	$ _____
Earnings from other/temporary job	$ _____
Sale of personal belongings	$ _____
Other (what or who?):	$ _____
Other (what or who?):	$ _____
Other (what or who?):	$ _____

Cash Flow Forecast

Try to include in your business plan a basic cash flow forecast for your company covering at least the first four to six weeks of operation. For any cash shortages your forecast may predict, state your plans for covering the shortages.

Even a potentially successful business can meet major difficulties or fail if it runs out of money to pay its bills and salaries on time. A good *cash flow forecast* helps avoid this common but serious business problem. A cash flow forecast estimates the cash that will be coming into the company and the cash that will be flowing out during a given time period. It is called a forecast because it makes *predictions* about the cash flow for a business.

One of the main purposes of a cash flow forecast is to predict whether the cash coming into the business over a given time will be enough to provide the cash the company must pay out during the same time. A cash flow forecast might show that sales will bring in a lot of cash in December, but during September and October the company can expect cash shortages. Knowing this, the entrepreneur can prepare for the predicted cash problems.

For example, the entrepreneur might arrange for temporary financing (a loan for a short time) to help the business through the shortages. The company could then pay off the short-term loan with the strong cash flow expected in December.

Larger entrepreneurial ventures usually need month-by-month cash flow forecasts that cover at least the first year of operation. Week-by-week cash flow forecasts can be more practical for smaller ventures. Use a chart like the one below to chart yours.

Week	1	2	3	4
1. Beginning cash balance				
Cash Receipts				
2. Cash sales receipts				
3. Invoice payments				
4. Other cash receipts				
5. Total Receipts				
Cash Disbursements				
6. Inventory/office supplies				
7. Employee payroll				
8. Rent, utilities, and telephone				
9. Advertising/promotion				
10. Consultants/promotional fees				
11. Other cash disbursements				
12. Total Disbursements				
13. Total Cash Flow				
14. Ending Cash Balance				

Revenue and Expenses

In casual conversation, you may hear people refer to operating expenses as "overhead."

As an entrepreneur, you will like the word *revenue.* Business people use that word to refer to the money that comes into their company. Revenue (or sales revenue) is the total dollar amount a company receives from the sales of its goods or services over a particular time period, such as a week, month, or year.

After start-up, a typical business must face two main categories of ongoing *expenses:* product costs and operating expenses.

Product costs, or "cost of goods sold," usually refer to the cost of the actual materials and labor used to produce the goods that are sold to customers. Product costs vary directly with the quantity of the goods that are produced. For example, if you were producing stackable wooden storage cubes, the amount of money you would have to spend on the wood, fasteners, paint, and labor to make the cubes would be your product costs. Your total product costs for a particular period—say, one month—would vary depending on whether you produced 12 cubes or 200 cubes that month.

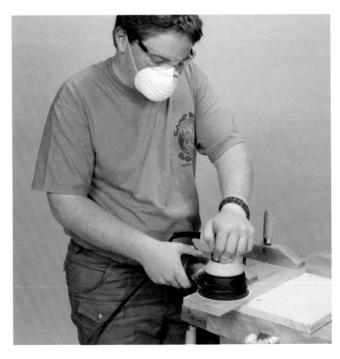

The additional costs that are required to cover the basic operation of the rest of the business are called *operating expenses.* Salaries, advertising, rent, utilities, and office supplies are typical operating expense categories.

Operating expenses are fixed—they do not vary directly with the quantity of the goods produced. For example, if you rented a small shop in which to make stackable wooden storage cubes, you would pay the same amount for rent every month whether you produced 12 cubes or 200 cubes in any particular month.

For a small service business that does not produce a physical item, it is common to ignore the idea of product costs and include all business expenses in the category of operating expenses. For simplicity, you may want to take the same approach if you start a service business.

Profit and Loss

If, over a period of time such as a year, the total revenue a business earns exceeds the total expenses (product costs plus operating expenses) the business pays out, the difference (revenue minus expenses) is called *profit.* Profit is the net income (before taxes) earned after covering all expenses.

Profits can be reinvested in the business to help it grow, distributed to the people who share ownership (you and your investors), directed toward a predetermined philanthropic cause, or divided among these options, according to your business plan.

If the total expenses the business pays out exceeds the revenue earned, then the difference (expenses minus revenue) is called a *loss.* To stay in business, the business would have to have enough money available to cover the loss.

In your business plan, you will want to forecast the potential profit or loss you expect for the company over the start-up period of operation. It is common for a business to show a loss during its early stages as the company establishes itself in the marketplace and begins to attract customers. Over time, however, the entrepreneur, and any lenders or investors, will want to see that the company is on the road to earning satisfactory profits in the future.

Pricing Your Product

You will have to decide on a price for the product or service you are going to sell. You can take several approaches to pricing. The following example shows one method you can use to establish a possible price after you have researched market demand, the prices competitors are charging, costs of materials and labor, operating expenses, forecasted sales, and desired profits.

Ray, a young entrepreneur, plans to sell T-shirts. Ray has calculated that his product costs (materials and labor) will be $10 per T-shirt (that is, per unit of production). Ray has also estimated that the total operating expenses for his business will be $50 a week (covering rent, utilities, telephone, advertising, loan payments, and license fees).

Suppose Ray's market research has led him to believe he can sell eight T-shirts in a week. To calculate his total product costs for one week, he multiplies the number of units (T-shirts) per week by the unit product cost: 8 x $10 = $80.

Next, he must set a target for the profit he wants the business to earn over the same period (one week). Assume that Ray decides he would like to earn a profit of $30 per week for the business to be worth the investment of resources he will be making.

Finally, Ray adds up the product costs, operating expenses, and profit forecasted for the week to calculate the total sales revenue needed to cover these three items. He then divides by the number of units he expects to sell to get the price per unit.

It is not unusual for an entrepreneur to increase price hoping to increase profits. In fact, total profits may decrease depending on how much less customers will buy at the higher price.

In this example, Ray's business sales over the course of a week must generate $80 to cover the product costs, $50 to cover the operating expenses, and $30 to cover the profit Ray would like to earn. That adds up to $160 of sales revenue that he needs to generate in one week. Dividing the weekly sales revenue needed ($160) by the number of units he believes he can sell in a week (8), Ray calculates $20 as the possible price for each T-shirt.

> $160 (Total sales revenue) ÷ 8 (Units sold)
> = $20 (Price per unit)

Following these steps is one way to establish a price you might charge for your product or service. There are many other possible approaches to pricing. Some can be as simple as doubling your product's cost of materials or cost of materials and labor or by checking out your competitors' prices and charging a little less.

You can see that there is a close relationship between price, costs and expenses, and the amount of profit. The entrepreneur must consider if the profit desired is realistic, based on the prices that can be charged, the business costs and expenses, and the sales that potentially can be made at those prices.

In general, no matter how they first establish a price, most entrepreneurs find they must adjust their initial pricing several times as they try to take into account the tug-of-war between such factors as the low prices competitors charge, the profit entrepreneurs want to make, and the quantities people are willing to buy at various prices. Keep in mind that as you test the potential results of different prices, you are seeking a price that will allow you to earn the most profit, based on the actual sales you can make in your market at that price and on the difference between revenue and total expenses at that price.

Pricing a Service

If you have a service rather than a product, the cost of your service often is expressed as an *hourly rate*—the amount of money you charge for one hour of your service. You can use a similar approach to set an initial price—or hourly rate—for your service. Add up your operating expenses and desired profit to find the total revenue needed from your service business during a period (such as one week). Then divide by the number of hours of service you believe you will provide to customers during that same week. The result of that calculation is a possible hourly rate you can charge for your service.

As you test the potential results of different hourly rates, your financial goal is the same as that of an entrepreneur selling a product. You are looking for that price (hourly rate) that will let your business earn the most profit.

Again, plan to adjust your initial hourly rate several times as you take into account the same issues as for product pricing—the tug-of-war between the low hourly rates competitors charge, the profit you wish to make, and the number of hours of service that people are willing to buy at various hourly rates.

Debt is money that must be repaid to its lender. The borrower also must make regular payments to the lender called *interest*—the price paid for using someone else's money.

Debt and Equity

Entrepreneurs often need financial help when they start up a company. If you expect your start-up costs to be more than you can finance personally, then you will have to get money from others to launch your new business. If you borrow the money for the business, that is referred to as *debt financing.*

The most typical debt financing for small businesses does not give the lender any ownership in the company, and the return to the lender is not based on the company's profits. The return to the lender is based on the interest rate that was established for the loan and the period of time over which the loan will be repaid.

A lender's interest in the health of the business is usually focused on the business's ability to pay the interest it owes to the lender on time, and to pay off the full amount of the loan when it is due. With debt financing, the entrepreneur is responsible for paying back the debt and interest even if there is no profit.

On the other hand, if an entrepreneur raises money from investors or partners in return for a share in the ownership (and therefore the profits or losses) of the company, that is referred to as *equity financing*. Those with *equity* in a company are part owners. The returns (earnings) to equity holders will be based on the success and the profits of the company. For this reason, equity holders will often take an active interest in all aspects of the company, its operation, and its future.

For example, if a relative invests money in your business as an equity holder, that family member will share in the ownership and business profits. If the same family member loans you money for your business, then you will owe the parent or relative the amount of the loan as a debt and will have to pay interest.

Sources of Money

Common sources of money include personal savings, family members, friends, a bank, partners, early forecasted earnings of the company (if the company is set to start making profits right away), a home equity loan, venture capitalists, and "angels."

A *venture capitalist* or a venture capital company can be a source of money for entrepreneurial ventures that are riskier than banks prefer. Banks generally avoid lending money to higher-risk ventures. Venture capitalists, however, if shown a good business plan for a good idea, may be willing to invest as equity partners. They may be willing to assume the higher risk if they have enough confidence that a new business will generate large returns in the future for its equity holders. However, venture capitalists fund only a tiny percentage of all new ventures.

An *angel* is typically a wealthy individual who—in selected cases—is willing to invest personal money in interesting, higher-risk business ventures with prospects of high returns in the future. In some cases, angels may be willing to provide funds simply to support promising new entrepreneurs, particularly if the angels themselves earned their wealth as entrepreneurs. That does not mean they are willing to make a bad investment just to be helpful. However, they might be willing to take a chance on a venture with higher-than-normal risk in the hope of helping a new entrepreneur—with a good idea and a good plan—to succeed.

One of the decisions you will make as an entrepreneur is whether you would rather share your ownership and profits *(equity financing)* or pay interest on a loan and eventually repay it *(debt financing).*

Moving Ahead to Start Your Business

You have created and reviewed your business plan. What are the results? Do you have a plan that you, and others, think will lead to a successful business? If so, congratulations and well done.

On the other hand, if your hard work has led you to conclude that your idea probably would not result in a successful business, congratulations also. It often takes just as much research, knowledge, and judgment for an entrepreneur to decide that a business idea will *not* work as it does to show that an idea *will* work. It is also more difficult to accept the results when your conclusion is, "This just is not going to fly."

During this first planning effort, you may have identified other possible opportunities. Explore their feasibility.

As you assess your business idea, be absolutely honest. Have you answered all of the key questions and gathered all of the important information you will need? Is that information telling you that you have a good idea that looks as if it will work? Or, is it telling you that your idea may not result in a successful business venture?

Your business plan should convince people that your idea will work or has a good chance of working. However, the first person that plan should convince is *you*.

If you have decided that your idea won't work, carefully review both the idea and the business plan. See if there are changes you could make that might lead to an idea that would work.

Making It Happen—What's Next?

Marketing is very important. Make sure you have a clear message you can deliver to the market to inform people about your business.

Let us assume you have determined your business idea is feasible and your business plan is complete. Several preliminary steps may be useful as you begin the start-up process.

Posters. Developing a poster to promote your business will encourage you to create the main message you want to communicate to the market about your product or service. It can lead you to design a logo or a particular "look" or image for your company. Once complete, a poster announces to the market the product or service you are providing.

Fliers. Fliers are printed papers that are used for mass advertising. This inexpensive sales tool communicates that you are in business and what you are offering for sale. In a flier, you can tell people about your product or service, its features and benefits, why they should be interested in buying it, the price, and any special offers you are making. Also include information about where and how people can get your product or service.

Think about the major points you want to make. Give most of the space in the flier to the most important point. Keep fliers short and make them immediately interesting. Most people will give a flier one to two seconds, at most, to catch their attention before throwing it away.

Through social media, users share information, ideas, personal messages, and other content via electronic communication. Several types of online communities could be a good fit for your business.

Social networks allow you to connect with other people of similar interests and backgrounds. Each user creates a profile and interacts with other users, both individually and as group members. Two examples are Facebook and LinkedIn.

Bookmarking sites allow users to save, organize, manage, and share links to various websites and resources. Delicious and StumbleUpon are two such services.

Social news sites let people post various news items or links to outside articles, and then users vote on favorite items. Voter favorites are featured more prominently. Examples include Digg and Reddit.

Media sharing lets users upload and share pictures and videos. Some sites feature profiles and comments. YouTube, Instagram, and Flickr are popular ones.

Microblogging services are short updates disseminated to subscribers. The most popular example is Twitter.

Blog comments and forums give members a place on the Web to hold conversations by posting messages concerning just about any topic of interest. Tumblr is one popular blog site and currently hosts over 13 million blogs.

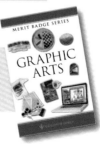

For more about writing and designing posters, fliers, and Web pages, see the *Graphic Arts* merit badge pamphlet.

Business Cards. Designing and producing a business card is usually a high priority for any budding entrepreneur. A business card is a highly versatile communication tool.

As an entrepreneur, you may view people you meet as potential buyers of your product or service, potential suppliers, professional consultants, or even potential partners and investors. Some may know other people who might be interested in your business. Leaving a business card with these people will enable them to contact you in the future or have others contact you.

The information normally found on a well-designed business card should include the name and address of your company, your contact information, company logo, and a brief line about your product or service.

Weigh the benefits of packing as much information as possible on a card against the risk of the card appearing cluttered and unprofessional. Try to find a good balance between the card's information and its overall visual appeal.

Specialty shops offer many different services to help you create a card and then produce it in large numbers at a reasonable cost. You can also use a computer, printer, and business-card sheets from an office supply store to design and print your own cards.

Discuss with your counselor which of the preliminary steps described—poster, flier, other sales tool, business card, or prototype—would be most helpful for your business idea. You might decide to do them all.

Prototypes. If you plan to produce a product rather than offer a service, an important early step is to create a *prototype*—a fully working model as a sample of the product you hope to eventually sell to customers. Building a prototype

- Is an excellent way to work out the "kinks"—the unexpected problems you are sure to face as you try to create a new product

- Will help you accurately estimate the cost of materials and labor to produce the product

- Gives you a tangible model to show potential customers and possible investors

- Will help prove that the concept you generated and researched for your business plan can, in fact, be physically produced—and that there really is an actual product that can work as described in the plan

A creative card can suggest a creative company. However, keep the card's message simple, clear, and easy to read.

Other Sales Tools

Write a **newspaper or radio advertisement** for your business. The longer the ad, the more expensive, so limit a newspaper ad to 50 words or fewer and a **radio advertisement** to under 10 seconds. Do your ads get attention? Will they make a potential customer want to buy the product? Did the ads give all the important information? Price? Phone number?

Design a **website** or **Web page** for your business. Emphasize your main sales message and describe your product or service, its features and benefits, how it meets customers' needs, the price, any special offers available, and ordering information.

Hand out your business card freely to all people who might be interested in your business's goods or services or who might want a business relationship with your company.

Shifting Into High Gear

With your best opportunity and idea identified, and your business plan and selected preliminary steps completed, your business start-up process can shift into high gear. You can move ahead with the many activities needed to begin your entrepreneurial venture. Some of the necessary activities include:

- Obtaining the money you need to cover start-up costs

- Preparing your service location or the location where you will produce your goods

- Acquiring a business license, name registration, or other necessary documents (See "Legal Matters," below.)

- Opening a company bank account

- Establishing the system you will use to keep records

- Putting together the best team of associates to help you (if your business will need the services of others)

- Identifying suppliers of materials and obtaining necessary resources

- Beginning production

- Marketing, marketing, marketing

Legal Matters

A business may need a special license or permit to operate legally. A permit might be required before you put up a sign to advertise your business. An entrepreneur may need to register a business name or a trademark, copyright, or patent. Taxes—sales taxes, payroll taxes, and income taxes—are other common concerns of small businesses and entrepreneurs.

Another starting point for information on licenses and permits is the U.S. Small Business Administration. See the resources section for more information.

Talk with your counselor, parent, partners, investors, or other knowledgeable people about the legal requirements you may have to cover as an entrepreneur. Every state has its own rules and regulations. City and county governments also have regulations on permits you may need. Space is too limited in this pamphlet to cover them all—you will have to do your own research.

A good place to start research on business permits is your city hall.

Also think about the legal structure of your business. Many entrepreneurs operate as *sole proprietors.* A sole proprietorship is owned by one person. It is the most popular business structure because it is easy to create and operate. Setting it up requires no legal documents or legal fees. You can operate under your own name or a business name—a "DBA," or "doing business as" company. You report any business income or loss on your personal income tax return.

A sole proprietor, however, is personally responsible for all the work, debts, and risk. If you are sued, you could lose not only your business assets, but also your personal belongings and money.

A *partnership*—another common legal structure among entrepreneurs—has the same sorts of risks. Each partner is personally responsible for the business's debts and liabilities. If the business is sued, the partners stand to lose their personal possessions and money as well as the assets of the business.

Requirement 4a(4) asks you to identify and describe the potential liability risks of your product or service. If you run a bike-repair business, for example, and a customer is hurt on a bike you just overhauled, you might be held liable for the person's medical expenses. If you are a pet-sitter and a valuable show or breeding animal gets sick or dies under your care, the owner might sue you for the value of the injured animal.

Liability refers to obligations or responsibilities under the law.

Does your product or service pose any potential liability risks? If so, you may need to purchase liability insurance to protect yourself and your business if you are sued.

Liability, licenses, permits, business registration, taxes, and all such matters can be complicated and even scary for the new entrepreneur. You will need professional advice. Maybe you can barter (trade) products or services with an attorney to help you work through these issues. Perhaps an attorney will donate his or her services to help your start-up venture. Law students at a nearby university might be able to help.

Be creative in seeking the legal advice you need. An entrepreneur's creativity is always getting a workout, in everything from product development to financing and marketing. Getting affordable legal advice and assistance is no exception.

This information on legal matters is provided to help you fulfill the requirements for the Entrepreneurship merit badge. It is not and should not be considered professional legal advice. For all legal questions related to launching and running your business, you should seek the advice of a qualified professional.

The best form of advertising is positive word-of-mouth from a job well done.

Business Ethics

Suppose you have a computer-service business and a customer wants you to install a pirated copy of a popular software program. If you make an illegal copy as the customer asks, you will be stealing from the owner of the copyright on that software. What will you do?

Suppose you and a partner agree to rent a space where you can set up and sell your wood carvings. The rent comes due. You pay your half, but your partner says he doesn't have the money for his share of the rent. Is that your problem? What is your obligation to the person who is renting you the space?

Suppose a customer says, "If you can make delivery of a dozen widgets by Wednesday, you've got a deal." You know you can't build and deliver a dozen widgets before Thursday at the earliest. To make the sale, do you promise what you can't deliver?

Bending the rules is bad business.

Questions of ethics arise in every business. To save money or to gain a competitive edge, entrepreneurs may be tempted to cut corners, bend the rules, or lower their standards. But cheat, lie, or betray a trust even once, and the damage to your reputation can be permanent. Customers and other business owners will shy away from doing business with someone who engages in unethical practices.

What are your ethical responsibilities in your business? Discuss with your counselor any ethical questions you have faced or think you may face in your venture. How do your moral principles or values affect your business decisions? Can you state, in two or three sentences, a personal code of ethics for yourself and your business? Or explain the values you follow when interacting with people in a business setting?

Is Your Dream Coming True?

Show everyone, including yourself, that you can make your business dream a reality. Once your business is under way, write a report on its status. Include interesting evidence of the steps you went through to plan and start the business. Also report on the performance of your business, including sales revenue, expenses, and profit or loss.

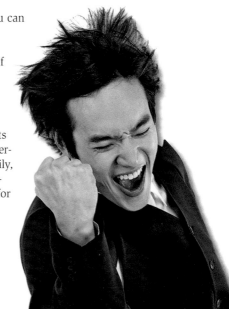

Share your experiences and your results with your counselor and others. Let your personal and business networks—friends, family, investors, professionals, and other entrepreneurs—know how you are doing, and ask for their feedback and advice. Work to make your business succeed and to achieve the goals you have set for it and for yourself.

The Big Picture

The work of an entrepreneur can be fulfilling and rewarding. Earning the Entrepreneurship merit badge will help you know whether being an entrepreneur is a career option that interests you.

Even if you do not plan to start your own business, you are now better able to decide which entrepreneurial skills and characteristics might help you along the path you do choose. You are also in a better position to change your mind later in life about becoming an entrepreneur, if you should choose to do so.

Look again at the section of this pamphlet on the roles and contributions of entrepreneurs in our society. Keep in mind all that is possible for those who are willing to identify opportunities, take the initiative (even when they cannot be sure of the results), and do their best to bring their ideas to reality.

Happy hunting—for opportunities!

Entrepreneurial Eagle Scout

Ewing Marion Kauffman was a highly successful entrepreneur and an Eagle Scout. He founded Marion Laboratories, a pharmaceutical and health-care company that was valued at more than $6 billion when it merged with Merrell Dow in 1989 to become the Marion Merrell Dow Corporation.

"Mr. K," as Mr. Kauffman was affectionately known, also endowed a $1 billion foundation—the Ewing Marion Kauffman Foundation—dedicated to a vision of self-sufficient people living in healthy communities. He believed that three key characteristics were vital to the ultimate success of the entrepreneur: sharing the rewards of entrepreneurship with those who produce, treating others as you would like to be treated, and giving back to your community.

May the future bring you the kind of entrepreneurial experiences and successes "Mr. K" had in mind. May you enjoy all of the great feelings that can come from setting goals, accomplishing tasks, achieving success, and bringing benefits to yourself and others.

Entrepreneurship Resources

Scouting Literature

American Business, Communication, Graphic Arts, Inventing, Personal Management, Public Speaking, and *Salesmanship* merit badge pamphlets, and any pamphlets related to your business venture, such as *Dog Care* and *Pets* for a pet-sitting service; *Gardening, Insect Study, Plant Science,* and *Soil and Water Conservation* for a lawn-and-garden business; etc. For a complete list, see the "Merit Badge Library" list on the inside of the back cover of this and other merit badge pamphlets.

Visit the Boy Scouts of America's official retail website (with your parent's permission) at www.scoutstuff.org for a complete listing of merit badge pamphlets and other helpful Scouting resources.

Books

Bochner, Arthur, Rose Bochner, and Adriane Berg. *The New Totally Awesome Business Book for Kids.* William Morrow Paperbacks, 2007.

———. *The New Totally Awesome Money Book for Kids,* 3rd ed. William Morrow Paperbacks, 2007.

Bernstein, Daryl, and Rob Husberg. *Better Than a Lemonade Stand!* Aladdin/Beyond Words, 2012.

Beroff, Art, and Terry Adams. *How to Be a Teenage Millionaire.* McGraw-Hill, 2000.

Cathers, Ben. *Conversations With Teen Entrepreneurs: Success Secrets of the Younger Generation.* iUniverse, 2003.

Collins, Robyn, and Kimberly Burleson Spinks. *Prepare to Be a Teen Millionaire.* HCI, 2008.

Ferguson Publishing Company staff. *Entrepreneurs,* 3rd ed. (Ferguson's *Careers in Focus.*) Ferguson Publishing, 2009.

Hansen, Mark Victor. *The Richest Kids in America: How They Earn It, How They Spend It, How You Can Too.* Hansen House Publishing, 2009.

Harper, Stephen C. *The McGraw-Hill Guide to Starting Your Own Business: A Step-by-Step Blueprint for the First-Time Entrepreneur.* McGraw-Hill, 2003.

Isaacson, Walter. *Steve Jobs.* Simon & Schuster, 2011.

Linecker, Adelia Cellini. *What Color Is Your Piggy Bank? Entrepreneurial Ideas for Self-Starting Kids.* Lobster Press, 2004.

Macarthy, Andrew. *500 Social Media Marketing Tips.* CreateSpace Independent Publishing Platform, 2013.

Mariotti, Steve. *The Young Entrepreneur's Guide to Starting and Running a Business.* Three Rivers Press, 2000.

Marlow, Kip. *The Entrepreneurs: Success and Sacrifice.* CreateSpace Independent Publishing Platform, 2013.

O'Neill, Jason. *Bitten by the Business Bug: Common Sense Tips for Business and Life From a Teen Entrepreneur.* CreateSpace Independent Publishing Platform 2010.

Rankin, Kenrya. *Start It Up.* Zest Books, 2011.

Schiffman, Stephan. *Young Entrepreneur's Guide to Business Terms.* Scholastic, 2003.

Scofield, Rupert. *The Social Entrepreneur's Handbook: How to Start, Build, and Run a Business That Improves the World.* McGraw Hill, 2011.

Topp, Carol. *Starting a Micro Business.* Ambassador Publishing, 2010.

Toren, Adam and Matthew. *Kidpreneurs: Young Entrepreneurs With Big Ideas!* Business Plus Media Group LLC, 2009.

Organizations and Websites
BizWorld
311 California St., Suite 750
San Francisco, CA 94104
Toll-free telephone: 888-424-9543
Website: http://www.bizworld.org

By Kids For Kids
1177 High Ridge Road
Stamford, CT 06905
Telephone: 203-321-1226
Website: http://www.bkfk.com

DECA
1908 Association Drive
Reston, VA 20191
Telephone: 703-860-5000
Website: http://www.deca.org

Entrepreneurs' Organization
500 Montgomery St., Suite 700
Alexandria, VA 22314-1437
Telephone: 703-519-6700
Website: http://www.eonetwork.org

Resources for Entrepreneurs
Ewing Marion Kauffman Foundation
4801 Rockhill Road
Kansas City, MO 64110
Telephone: 816-932-1000
Website: http://www.entrepreneurship.org

Future Business Leaders of America—Phi Beta Lambda
1912 Association Drive
Reston, VA 20191-1591
Toll-free telephone: 800-325-2946
Website: http://www.fbla-pbl.org

Inc. Magazine
7 World Trade Center
New York, NY 10007-2195
Telephone: 212-389-5377
Website: http://www.inc.com

Junior Achievement
One Education Way
Colorado Springs, CO 80906
Telephone: 719-540-8000
Website: http://www.ja.org

SCORE Association

409 3rd St., SW, Suite 100A
Washington, DC 20024
Toll-free telephone: 800-634-0245
Website: http://www.score.org

TeenStartUps.com

Entrepreneur Media Inc.
2445 McCabe Way, Suite 400
Irvine, CA 92614
Telephone: 949-261-2325
Website:
http://www.entrepreneur.com/tsu

U.S. Small Business Administration

409 Third St., SW
Washington, DC 20416
Toll-free telephone: 800-827-5722
Website: http://www.sba.gov

YoungBiz

40 Wall St.
The Trump Building, 28th floor
New York, NY 10005
Toll-free telephone: 800-878-4982
Website: http://www.youngbiz.com

Youth Venture

1700 North Moore St., Suite 2000
Arlington, VA 22209
Telephone: 703-527-8300
Website: http://www.youthventure.org

Acknowledgments

For reviewing and suggesting updates to both the requirements and contents for the 2013 revised edition of this pamphlet, the Boy Scouts of America thanks David Ehrlich. Mr. Ehrlich is a business/marketing teacher at Milford High School in Highland, Michigan. In addition, he is a group leader on the BSA Merit Badge Maintenance Task Force.

For the 2005 revisions, the BSA appreciates the efforts of Joe Denekamp, Ph.D. Dr. Denekamp is a professor at Indiana University's Kelley School of Business and director of the Young Entrepreneur's Association.

The BSA also thanks the Center for Entrepreneurial Leadership Inc. of the Ewing Marion Kauffman Foundation for its generous grant to fund the development of the Entrepreneurship merit badge requirements and the first edition of this pamphlet. Additional thanks to the original author, Marilyn Kourilsky, formerly of the Center for Entrepreneurial Leadership, Ewing Marion Kauffman Foundation; Gary Rabbior of the Canadian Foundation for Economic Education; and Scott J. Shickler.

The Boy Scouts of America is grateful to the men and women serving on the Merit Badge Maintenance Task Force for the improvements made in updating this pamphlet.

Photo and Illustration Credits

Wally Amos, courtesy—page 17 *(left)*

Dell Computer Corporation, courtesy—page 17 *(right)*

Google.com, courtesy—page 17 *(center)*

©Jupiterimages.com—pages 14, 16 *(bottom)*, and 62

©Photos.com—cover *(all except merit badge, business card)*; pages 3, 7, 10 *(inset)*, 11, 16 *(top)*, 20 *(inset)*, 23 *(bottom right)*, 33, 34 *(bottom)*, 41–42 *(both)*, 47 *(top)*, 49, 57, 65–66 *(both)*, 69, 73, 76, and 89

Wikipedia.org/Matthew Morven, courtesy—page 60

All other photos and illustrations not mentioned above are the property of or are protected by the Boy Scouts of America.

Dan Bryant—page 34 *(top)*

Darrell Byers—page 13 *(top right)*

Daniel Giles—pages 22, 43, and 46

Brian Payne—pages 9 *(top)*, 10 *(main)*, 13 *(left)*, 50 *(both)*, 54–56 *(all)*, 58 *(top)*, 70, 74 *(top)*, 78 *(top, center)*, and 87

Randy Piland—pages 13 *(bottom right)*, 30, 35, 37, 40, 61, and 78 *(bottom)*

Notes